THE LOVING PARENT GUIDEBOOK

STRATEGIES TO BREAK FREE FROM EMOTIONAL DEPENDENCY

JOYFUL BOFEST

Click on this link to view more and access books or scan the code thanks

https://www.amazon.com/author/bofest4eal

COPYRIGHT © 2024
BY JOYFUL BOFEST

The information provided in this book is for educational and informational purposes only. It is not intended to be a substitute for professional advice, diagnosis, or treatment. Readers are advised to seek the guidance of qualified professionals regarding their specific situations.

Disclaimer: The author and publisher of this book have made every effort to ensure the accuracy of the information presented herein. However, they assume no responsibility for errors or omissions, or for any damages resulting from the use of the information contained in this book. Readers are solely responsible for their own actions and decisions.

GRATITUDE

My deepest gratitude goes out to everyone who contributed to the creation of this book. To begin with, I would like to thank my family for all of their help and encouragement during this trip. Your compassion and kindness have been my greatest sources of support. My editor, Michael, deserves a great deal of credit for his insightful feedback and guidance in shaping this book into its final form. We express our sincere gratitude to my children for their insightful insights and significant contributions to the book.

Thank you to everyone who shared their stories and experiences with me. Your audacity and persistence have really impressed me. Lastly, I just wanted to say thank you to all of the readers who are coming along for the ride. I really hope that you find hope and healing in this book. I am appreciative.

APPLICATION OF THIS BOOK

This is "The Loving Parent Guidebook: Discovering Your Inner Teenage." For anyone seeking personal growth and healing after being impacted by emotionally immature parents, this book is meant to be a helpful resource.

1. **Start with an overview.**

   Commence by reflecting on your own emotions and past encounters. Take some time to jot down notes in your notebook or reflect on the concepts discussed in each chapter.

2. **Take part in the activities.**

   This book offers a range of exercises and activities designed to help you explore your thoughts and feelings. Pay close attention to these   exercises.

3. **Use the techniques and tools**.

Throughout the chapters, you will discover practical resources and techniques that you may use to fix and restore. Examine how incorporating these strategies into your daily routine affects your general well-being.

4. *Seek assistance.*

The fallout from parenting, which lacks emotional maturity, should not be experienced by you alone. It might take some time to recover from its effects. Consider seeking help from a therapist, a support group, or a reliable friend   or   relative.

5. **Go at your own pace.**

   Remember that healing is a process, and taking your time is OK. Remind yourself to be kind and patient with yourself throughout this process.

6. **Access the book again as needed.**

   You might use this book as a useful resource whenever you need guidance or inspiration. Don't hesitate to review chapters or activities as needed on your journey to healing and self-discovery.

7. **Discuss your ideas**

   Consider sharing your views and experiences with others if it makes you feel good. Your adventure may inspire and motivate others on a similar path.

TABLE OF CONTENTS

OVERVIEW

Acknowledging Emotional Unstable Behavior Emotionally immature conduct may take many different forms, and it impacts not just the one displaying it but also others around them, particularly their children. In this section, we will look at the characteristics and effects of emotional immaturity, emphasizing the significant effects it has on adult offspring.

IMPACT ON GROWN-UP DEPARTURES

Adult children of emotionally immature parents often have to navigate a difficult emotional landscape that is rife with rejection, inconsistent behavior, and emotional neglect. These interactions could have a long-term effect on their sense of self, interpersonal relationships, and overall   well-being.

SIGN RECOGNITION

Parents who are emotionally immature may display characteristics such as emotional instability, a deficiency in empathy, or an incapacity to regulate their own feelings. Recognizing these signs may help adult children understand the fundamental causes of their upbringing and the impact it has had on their lives.

A DYSFUNCTIONAL CYCLE

Children raised by emotionally immature parents may continue this cycle in their relationships and personal lives. If no help is provided, they risk passing on bad behavioral tendencies to future generations.

UNBREAKABLE

Knowledge, however, is the first step in the healing process. Admitting that their parents were emotionally immature and how it influenced their lives might help adult children break out of the dysfunctional cycle and reclaim emotional autonomy.

CHAPTER ONE
UNDERSTANDING EMOTIONAL IMMATURITY

Emotionally immature behavior may take many different forms and impact not just the person displaying it but also others around them, particularly their children. In this section, we will look at the characteristics and effects of emotional immaturity, emphasizing the significant effects it has on adult offspring.

Impact on Grown-Up Departures

Adult children of emotionally immature parents often have to navigate a difficult emotional landscape that is rife with rejection, inconsistent behavior, and emotional neglect. These interactions could have a long-term effect on their sense of self, interpersonal relationships, and overall well-being.

A Letter of Acknowledgment

Emotionally immature parents may display characteristics like emotional instability, a lack of empathy, or an inability to regulate their own feelings. Recognizing these signs may help adult children understand the fundamental causes of their upbringing and the impact it has had on their lives.

Emotionally immature parents may cause their children to grow up in a dysfunctional cycle that they may carry into their own relationships and lives. If no help is provided, they risk passing on bad behavioral tendencies to future generations. Unbreakable: However, awareness is the first step on the road to recovery. Admitting that their parents were emotionally immature and how it influenced their lives might help adult children break out of the dysfunctional cycle and reclaim emotional autonomy.

Emotionally immature parents' effects on their adult children's lives

The impact of emotionally immature parents on their adult children's lives is profound and multifaceted. This section will look at the ways that parents' behavior demonstrates emotional immaturity and the possible long-term effects on their kids.

Emotional incompetence and appraisal of circumstances

Emotionally immature parents may find it challenging to provide their children with the attention and support they need to thrive. Parents who disregard or minimize their children's experiences and feelings may be doing so because of their own emotional deficiencies, which make the children feel insignificant, invisible, and unseen.

Adequacy of Maladaptive Coping Methods

Due to a lack of emotional support and validation, children raised in emotionally immature environments may develop maladaptive coping mechanisms. These might include suppressing one's emotions, seeking validation from other people, or behaving in a manner that appeals to others.

Impact on Self-Esteem and Self-Respect

Children raised by emotionally immature parents may grow up believing that their wants and feelings are unjustified and unworthy of attention. This might lead to low self-esteem, a strong sense of inadequacy, and difficulty establishing healthy boundaries in relationships.

Habitually forming healthy connections

The unhealthy behaviors ingrained in children may carry over into adulthood, making it challenging for adult children of emotionally immature parents to build and maintain healthy relationships. They may struggle with communication, intimacy, and trust, which often reflect the dynamics they experienced in their first family.

Parting the Loop

Despite the challenges they face, adult children of emotionally immature parents have the opportunity to break out of the dysfunctional cycle and lead better, more fulfilling lives. Through self-awareness, therapy, and intentional healing work, people may learn to recognize and face the damaging patterns they inherited from their childhood, potentially leading to increased emotional resilience and well-being.

Recognizing and identifying emotionally inappropriate parents

The first step in understanding and moving beyond their upbringing is for adult children to acknowledge the emotional immaturity of their parents. In this part, we'll examine the key characteristics and behaviors that may indicate emotional immaturity in parents.

Inadequate emotional intelligence and autonomy

It may be difficult for immature parents to identify and regulate their own emotions. They may react impulsively, displaying anxiety, withdrawal, or wrath when they are stressed or angry, without considering the impact on their children.

Impredicable Or Changing Activities

Emotionally immature parents might act erratically or inconsistently, shifting between overly involved and negligent behavior.

This disparity may cause kids to feel unsure, perplexed, and uncomfortable about their parents.

Feeling compassionate for their children, but failing at it Empathy is a necessary component of good parenting, yet emotionally immature parents may find it challenging to empathize with their children's experiences. They may downplay or ignore their children's feelings, which would invalidate them and make them feel less valuable.

Understand that they will provide emotional support.

When a parent lacks emotional maturity, they may turn to their children for emotional support, seeing them less as dependents and more as pals or confidants. This reversal of roles might overburden children by placing an undue emphasis on adult responsibilities and endangering their emotional development.

Avoidance of Development or Modification

Emotionally immature parents may find it difficult to acknowledge their own shortcomings or to seek help in improving their parenting methods. Parents who are resistant to evolving or changing in response to their children's needs may obstinately uphold archaic parenting methods or ideologies.

Trouble Determining And Restoring Boundaries

Setting reasonable boundaries is essential to fostering dignity and independence in the parent-child relationship. Emotionally immature parents may find it challenging to set and maintain appropriate limits for their kids, either by abusing their power or by ignoring them.

Their Offspring's Parent

The behavior of emotionally immature parents expecting their children to do chores and fulfill obligations beyond their developmental stage is known as parentification. This might include acting as stand-in spouses when a partner is unavailable, mediators, or emotional support networks.

The experience of relating to an emotionally immature parent

Relationships with emotionally immature parents may be complicated and difficult, and they can have a significant impact on how adult children perceive their own emotions. In this part, we will look at the typical emotions and experiences that come up in relationships with emotionally immature parents.

Doubt and ambiguity: Relationships with adult children of emotionally immature parents are often fraught with doubt and ambiguity. Their parents' erratic or inconsistent conduct might make children wonder where they stand or what to anticipate.

Invalidated Emotions: Parents who lack emotional maturity may find it difficult to acknowledge or accept their kids' emotions, which leads to them being minimized or disregarded. As a result, adult children may internalize the idea that their emotions are insignificant or unworthy of attention, causing them to feel invalidated and self-conscious.

Emotional Rollercoaster: Adult children who have emotionally immature parents may experience abrupt highs and lows in their relationships that leave them feeling anxious and overwhelmed. The relationship may seem unstable and anxious due to their parents' strong emotions and erratic behavior.

Guilt and responsibility: In their connections with emotionally immature parents, adult children may experience feelings of guilt or responsibility. They often believe that they are accountable for their parents' happiness or well-being. As adult children attempt to strike a balance between their own demands and their parents', this sense of obligation may cause sentiments of self-sacrifice or anger.

Loneliness and Isolation: Even if they live with their parents, adult children of emotionally immature parents may experience extreme feelings of isolation and loneliness. They may feel emotionally estranged and alone if their parents are unable to establish a genuine emotional connection with them or provide substantial assistance.

Desiring Confirmation and Acceptance: In relationships with emotionally immature parents, wanting affirmation and acceptance is one of the most prevalent emotions. Adult children may long for their parents' love and approval, looking for validation in their actions or accomplishments to win their affection.

The four types of parents who lack emotional development

Parents' emotional immaturity may take many different forms, and each has a different effect on the connection between the parent and the child.

This section will examine four prevalent categories of parents that lack emotional maturity and the traits that set them apart.

The Parent Who Is Far Away

The absentee parent is not active in their child's life and is emotionally distanced from them. They could put their own wants and desires before their kids', which would make the kids feel ignored, irrelevant, and emotionally malnourished.

The Parent Who Is Entangled

The enmeshed parent is overly committed and entangled in their child's life, blurring boundaries and preventing the youngster from growing into an autonomous, self-aware adult. Their dependence on their child for emotional support and validation could result in a situation where the parent's needs take precedence over the child's needs.

The Pessimistic Parent

A critical parent is harsh, judgmental, and unduly critical of their child's actions, emotions, and ideas. Parental nitpicking, criticism, or belittling may cause a child's self-esteem to be undermined and inculcate feelings of shame and inadequacy.

The Self-Involved Parent

The self-involved parent is preoccupied with their own needs, desires, and interests, often at the expense of their child's well-being. They may lack empathy and consideration for their child's feelings, viewing them as extensions of themselves rather than individuals with their own unique needs and experiences.

CHAPTER TWO
20 STRATEGIES TO BREAK FREE FROM EMOTIONAL DEPENDENCY

Self-Awareness: Identify and admit emotional dependence tendencies in your relationships. identifying, for example, a propensity to continuously look to other people for validation or approval.

Identify triggers: recognize the circumstances or sentiments that lead to feelings of reliance. For example, realizing that when your lover hangs out with friends without you, it makes you feel insecure.

Set limits: To safeguard your autonomy and mental health, set up appropriate limits. Giving a buddy the space you need while they depend on you for emotional support is one way to demonstrate this.

Build self-esteem: Foster a solid feeling of confidence and self-worth that is unaffected by approval from others. Recognizing your own accomplishments and attributes, for instance, without looking to others for approval.

Practice self-care: Give your mind, body, and soul the nourishment they need. Make self-care a priority. This might include setting aside time for leisure activities, physical activity, rest, or alone time.

Seek therapy: To investigate underlying concerns and acquire coping mechanisms, think about attending therapy or counseling. For example, going to therapy to deal with early trauma that might be causing emotions of emotional reliance.

Confront negative ideas: Negative self-perceptions and feelings of worthiness should be questioned and challenged. For instance, put the notion that you are undeserving of love or acceptance to rest.

Embrace Independence: Develop your independence by pursuing interests, ambitions, and pastimes that bring you joy. This may be picking up a new pastime or working on a passion project on your own.

Establish support relationships: Be in the company of family and friends who uplift you and foster your development. An example would be confiding in a reliable friend about your difficulties and getting support and understanding in return.

Mindful Awareness: Engage in mindfulness exercises to accept and notice your feelings without passing judgment. For example, mindfulness meditation can help you watch dependency-related emotions without getting sucked into them.

Emotional Regulation: Develop healthy, independent coping mechanisms for your emotions. To process emotions on your own, you may try writing or using relaxation methods.

Dominance: To politely and effectively communicate your demands and desires, engage in assertive communication. For example, politely state your boundaries to a spouse who frequently controls the conversation.

Develop Coping Skills: Overcome obstacles and setbacks by strengthening your resilience through coping skill development. One such skill may be developing good coping skills for stressful situations, such as deep breathing or encouraging self-talk.

Tackle Codependent Behaviors: Recognize and address actions that support or maintain emotional dependence. This could include identifying and redefining actions like people-pleasing or overly attentive conduct.

Examine Different Attachment Styles: Recognize the effects of your attachment style on your interpersonal interactions. For example, identifying nervous attachment patterns and the ways in which they engender feelings of reliance.

Make gratitude a practice. To be fulfilled, practice being grateful for all of life's events and gifts. One way to practice this is to keep a gratitude notebook and list three things every day for which you are thankful.

Pay attention to personal development: Establish objectives for yourself and concentrate on ongoing development. For example, setting goals to acquire new skills or pursue independent study.

Establish healthy routines: Create routines in your life that support stability, balance, and wellbeing. Developing a daily schedule that allots time for work, rest, socializing, and self-care might be one way to do this.

Forgive Yourself: Show compassion for yourself and extend forgiveness to yourself for previous transgressions or perceived inadequacies. For example, engaging in self-forgiveness means extending your stay in a bad relationship beyond what was reasonable.

Celebrate Independence: Honor your accomplishments and advancements in severing your emotional attachment to others. This might be recognizing and appreciating any independent moments, no matter how little they may seem.

Recreation and Parenting

Reflection and development are the paths to overcoming the suffering caused by parents who lack emotional maturity. In this part, we'll discuss reparenting and healing—a process that helps adult children take back emotional control and enhances their relationships with others and with themselves.

Recognizing the suffering and agony caused by emotionally immature parents is the first step toward healing. This may include confronting difficult emotions such as grief, rage, and loss, as well as admitting how one's upbringing impacted their adult life.

To repair emotional immaturity, self-compassion must be developed. Regardless of how they were raised, adult children need to learn to love and accept who they are. They must learn to be understanding, kind, and accepting of themselves.

Establishing boundaries is crucial for maintaining healthy relationships and preserving one's mental health. When it comes to their parents and other individuals who could annoy them, adult children need to learn how to recognize their needs, speak up for them with confidence, and create boundaries. Reparenting is embracing and providing for one's wounded, defenseless inner child, who yearns for love and acceptance. By engaging with their inner children, practicing self-soothing skills, and having compassionate talks with themselves, adult children may provide the love and support that they may not have had as children. It might be difficult to recover from the effects of emotional immaturity; therefore, it's important to get help from therapists, close family members, or trustworthy friends. Seeking professional therapy may provide a secure environment for addressing previous traumas, creating coping mechanisms, and acquiring positive social skills.

Forgiveness is one of the most effective therapy strategies for adult children to help them let go of their bitterness and hatred toward their emotionally immature parents. Rather than relieving someone of the weight of harboring resentment and grudges, forgiveness sets them free from the past. It doesn't support or excuse past actions.

Healing emotional immaturity requires a continuous process of introspection and development. Adult children have the chance to rediscover their sense of self and purpose outside of their upbringing by exploring their ideas, interests, and hobbies.

Identifying a parent who lacks emotional maturity

Steer clear of emotionally immature parent-child interactions; they may be liberating as well as hard.

In this section, we'll talk about self-defense and preserving emotional distance from emotionally immature parents. Identify the causes. If you are aware of emotionally immature parents, you may prevent yourself from becoming their puppets.

Take note of the circumstances, acts, or remarks that often lead to codependent inclinations or strong emotional responses.

Apply emotional distance to your work. Keep your distance from your parents' feelings, ideas, and actions on an emotional level. Remember that their actions are not indicative of your character; rather, they are a reflection of their own emotional immaturity.

Set definite boundaries. With your parents, set and uphold boundaries that will protect your mental health. Be careful to clearly and consistently communicate your limits, and be ready to sue someone if they are crossed.

Cut off communication if required. You may want to think about cutting down on contact or setting aside time if you frequently feel stressed or worn out after dealing with an emotionally immature parent.

Make an effort to surround yourself with friends, family, or therapists—people who can validate and support you on an emotional level.

Take care of yourself. Prioritize self-care routines that support your mental, emotional, and physical well-being. Pursue cheerful, calm, and fulfilling activities, and make time each day for self-care.

CAD Documentation System When you're with your parents, you should learn effective coping mechanisms to deal with tension, worry, and other difficult feelings that could surface. This includes journaling, mindfulness meditation, and deep breathing exercises.

Seek out expert support. It could be a good idea to think about getting help from a therapist or counselor who can provide you with direction, affirmation, and coping mechanisms specific to your situation. Therapy may provide a secure setting where you can work on assertiveness, process your emotions, and mend old scars.

Grow in forgiveness and empathy. Although it's important to shield oneself from emotionally stressful relationships, make an effort to develop more empathy and forgiveness for your parents. Keep in mind that their actions can stem from internal trauma and unresolved grief.

Laying the groundwork for parenting

Giving oneself the love, acceptance, and support that one may not have had as a kid is essential to tending to one's wounded inner child.

This section will cover the fundamental procedures for starting reparenting and developing a loving and compassionate relationship with oneself.

To begin, examine yourself and your past to see if there were any instances of abuse or neglect during your early years. Think about the demands on you, your emotional requirements, and any recurrent behavioral patterns that may have started in your early years.

Embrace and validate the feelings and experiences that come from your inner child. Offer yourself the empathy, understanding, and approval that you may have longed for but were denied throughout your early years. The only way to cultivate self-compassion is to be kind, accepting, and understanding of yourself. While you face the difficulties of recovery and development, remind yourself that you are worthy of love and acceptance just by being human.

Be gentle with yourself. Give yourself the affection and encouragement that you may not have received as a youngster.

To calm your inner child, try self-soothing activities like curling up with a blanket, having a warm bath, or doing relaxation exercises.

To protect your mental well-being and respect your wants and desires, establish and maintain reasonable limits. Prioritize and set your own objectives first. Learn to say no to relationships or circumstances that are not beneficial to you.

Try these activities and methods for connecting with and nurturing your inner child. Through writing, sketching, or other creative expression, you may discover and mend the shattered bits of who you are yourself. If you are finding reparenting to be challenging, you may want to think about getting help from a support group, counselor, or therapist. They might provide you with direction, validation, and assistance. Be surrounded by people who understand and encourage your recovery process.

Self-healing is a slow, continuous process that calls for patience, perseverance, and dedication. There will be ups and downs throughout the recovery process, so remember to treat yourself with kindness and acknowledge your little accomplishments.

Rising Your Painful Dad

You may use your innate capacity for compassion, caring, and self-care to awaken your loving parent by providing yourself with the love and support you may have missed out on as a kid.

This section will provide realistic strategies for reawakening your inner loving parent and cultivating a more sympathetic and caring relationship with oneself. Learn to be kind to yourself.

Treat yourself with the same acceptance, tolerance, and kindness that you would provide to a close friend as you begin by engaging in self-compassion exercises.

Talk to yourself in a kind, supportive, and encouraging way, reminding yourself that you are worthy of love and compassion just for being human.

Self-Care Methods

Prioritize self-care practices that nourish and revitalize your body, mind, and spirit. Engage in happy, relaxing, and satisfying activities; they might be yoga, hiking in the woods, or your favorite past time.

Accept the kid within you. Take care of your inner child by reaching out to them and offering yourself the support, love, and encouragement you may not have had as a kid. Engage in enjoyable, imaginative, and creative activities that fulfill the desires and requirements of your inner child.

Gloriating Limits Set

Set and uphold compassionate boundaries to protect your mental well-being and honor your desires and choices. Learn to say no to situations or relationships that do not suit your best interests, and learn to prioritize your own needs and goals with kindness and compassion.

Make use of your pardon. By forgiving yourself and others, you can release yourself from any resentment, anger, or judgment that may be holding you back. Remember that giving yourself permission to forgive is a gift that will free you from the burden of carrying grudges and allow you to go on with kindness and grace.

Cultivated Thanksgiving

Focusing on all the blessings and richness in your life can help you cultivate an attitude of appreciation. Set aside some time each day to reflect on all the things, no matter how little, for which you are grateful, and allow that gratitude to nourish your heart and soul. Seek out resources and assistance. Seek connections and support from others who can provide you with words of wisdom, empathy, and affirmation on your path to finding your adoptive parent. Talk to others who are sympathetic and understanding about your experiences and ideas while you heal. Keep yourself surrounded by positive and motivating individuals.

CHAPTER THREE
BUILDING CONSISTENT RELATIONSHIPS

A strong family structure may serve as a guide for self-healing and creating a nurturing environment inside. This section will cover strong family dynamics and foundations that are relevant to the reparenting process.

Unconditional acceptance and love

Acceptance and love are readily provided in a happy family. Family members cherish and accept one another in spite of their flaws and mistakes. "Reparenting" is the practice of treating oneself with the same acceptance and love that you would provide to a cherished family member. It is about discovering how to appreciate and accept who you are.

Fair and open discussion

Honesty, respect, and open communication are characteristics of happy families. Family members may communicate their desires without fear of judgment or criticism. Learning to speak honestly and freely with oneself, to listen to your inner voice with care and curiosity, and to express your thoughts and feelings in a real and authentic manner are all essential skills for being a parent again.

Restrictions And Respect

Everybody in a happy family knows the rules and follows them. Establishing boundaries protects each person's independence and well-being while fostering respect and understanding between parties. Being aware of one's wants, setting and maintaining healthy boundaries with oneself, and loving and respecting oneself are all part of being a parent.

Families that are happy and healthy support and encourage one another. They share in one another's successes, provide support and encouragement when things get tough, and offer guidance and help when needed. Reparenting is treating oneself with kindness and support, accepting your strengths and successes, and providing yourself with comfort and self-assurance during trying times.

Disagreements are addressed politely and resolved with empathy in a happy family. Family members listen to one another, communicate honestly, and work together to find solutions that work for everyone. Reparenting means letting go of criticism of oneself and others, accepting forgiveness as a tool for healing and personal growth, and using love and forgiveness to solve underlying   issues.

Families that are happier prioritize harmony, enjoyment, and camaraderie. Providing opportunities for fun, conversation, and experience exchanges makes family members feel more bonded and included in the group. Being a parent again entails doing things that bring you happiness and fulfillment, fostering pleasure and connection within yourself, and developing an inner sense of connection and belonging.

A Model of Excellent Parenting

An   Example   of   Reparenting Replicating the dynamics of a happy family serves as a successful model for self-love, self-repair, acceptance, and emotional healing. In this part, we'll talk about how maintaining strong family values may help with reparenting.

Healthy families provide an environment where care is fostered in those who are open to receiving love and acceptance. Reparenting, on the other hand, means treating yourself with the same degree of unshakable support and compassion that you do for others, while embracing and appreciating every part of who you are without any limits or reservations.

Happy homes place great importance on these characteristics. Establishing a secure and embracing atmosphere for oneself to openly express wants, feelings, and ideas is referred to as "reparenting." This method assists you in creating a caring and loving relationship with yourself.

Families that are harmonious encourage each member's feeling of autonomy and dignity. Setting and maintaining personal boundaries, putting your health first, and firmly but kindly advocating for yourself are all part of being a parent.

The cornerstones of a healthy family dynamic are encouragement and support. Reparenting, on the other hand, is being kind, encouraging, and positive toward oneself in order to develop into a person who can console and support you through both achievements and failures.

Harmonious families highly value these processes and resolve conflicts in a kind and understanding manner. Reparenting entails forgiving oneself for mistakes and traumas, letting go of one's own judgment, and fostering harmony and inner serenity.

Joy and intimacy are fostered in happy families through in-depth conversations and common experiences. Reparenting includes taking care of oneself, developing a closer relationship with one's inner self, and nurturing a sense of fulfillment and connection inside.

Mindfulness's Importance in Parental Care

Awareness is an essential skill for loving parents. It could have a big impact on how we care for and feed ourselves throughout the reparenting process. Being conscious is not just a method; it's a way of being. Let us explore mindfulness's position as an essential tool in greater depth, with examples and firsthand testimonials from individuals who have directly experienced mindfulness's transforming potential.

Sarah is a prime example of this. Because of her past emotional abuse, she was anxious and judgmental of herself. Thanks to mindfulness meditation, she was able to objectively evaluate her ideas and emotions. As she continued to practice present-moment awareness, her perspective started to shift. By gently bringing her focus back to the present, she may find inner clarity and serenity instead of letting her negative self-talk get the best of her.

Let's look at Alex. His perfectionism and self-doubt were fostered by the criticism he had experienced as a child. He was able to practice mindfulness-based self-compassion, which allowed him to treat himself with compassion and love. When faced with losses or failures, he would persuade himself that everyone had problems and that he was deserving of love and compassion, just as he would a friend in need.

Learn about Maya, a person who had intense emotions and mood swings due to traumatic experiences in her life. She discovered that by practicing mindfulness techniques like the "RAIN" meditation (recognizing, accepting, investigating, and non-identifying), she was able to observe her emotions without being dominated by them. When she allowed herself to sit with discomfort and observe it with curiosity instead of resistance, she found that the power of her emotions gradually diminished, enabling her to respond to challenging situations with more resilience and clarity.

John felt detached and alone; mindfulness practices that encouraged a stronger connection with oneself brought him solace. He became adept at using techniques such as body scan meditations and mindful breathing to tune into his body's sensations and patterns. As he gained this inner knowledge, he felt a deep sense of connection to himself and had long-desired moments of tranquility and fulfillment.

Think of Emily, who had interpersonal problems and a tendency toward self-destruction. She used mindfulness writing to explore the underlying thoughts and emotions that drove her behavior. As she wrote about her experiences with compassion and curiosity, she discovered a great deal about the reasons for her habits and how they influenced her life. Because of her introspection, she was able to make thoughtful choices that were consistent with her objectives and values.

Consider David, who was always overwhelmed with his family's and career's responsibilities and felt burned out. He was able to find some peace in the midst of his busy life by engaging in regular mindfulness practices. He found that by making time every day for presence and stillness, he was able to reduce his stress levels and feel more anchored and in charge of his life. His newly discovered sense of well-being improved his relationships and activities, raising his overall quality of life.

CHAPTER FOUR
ADVANCED TECHNOLOGY IN REPARENTING

Transformation is the process of changing deeply rooted habits, attitudes, and behaviors in order to build a more supportive and loving connection with oneself. On this path to change, the following methods and approaches might be helpful:

Practice self-compassion on a regular basis to develop empathy and understanding for yourself. Recognise your intrinsic humanity and worth through self-directed exercises or guided meditations, while also offering consoling and supportive words. For instance, Sarah uses the mantras "May I be kind to myself in moments of struggle" or "May I embrace my imperfections with compassion and acceptance" in her regular self-compassion meditation sessions. This practice teaches her how to calm herself with compassion and tenderness, resulting in more self-acceptance and self-love.

Investigate inner child work methods to help establish a connection with your injured parts. To establish a connection with your inner child and provide consolation, support, and encouragement, try writing, visualizing, or doing art. One such individual is Alex, who sets aside time each week to write about his early years and have imaginary conversations with the person he was then. This is what we call "inner child labor." Through this process, he has the ability to move beyond his past traumas and give himself the love and acceptance that he so desperately needed as a young child.

Cognitive restructuring is the process of rethinking and confronting unfavorable concepts and thought patterns that contribute to feelings of inadequacy or self-doubt. Employ cognitive restructuring strategies to recognize and replace harmful thinking patterns with more realistic and compassionate ones. For example, Maya observes that she constantly criticizes herself and aspires to be flawless. Perhaps she might question herself, "Is this thought helpful or accurate?" to begin challenging these ideas. and swapping them out with arguments that are more logical, such as "I am a human and I have the right to make mimistakes." " work does not determine who I am." In your subconscious mind, plant ideas of empowerment, self-love, and self-worthiness.

To strengthen your beliefs, repeat encouraging statements loudly or quietly on a regular basis. For instance, John makes a list of affirmations that he believes will help him feel loved, accepted, and confident. By repeating these affirmations often, he helps them become ingrained in his memory and progressively transforms how he views himself. To help you shift your perspective and focus on the things in your life for which you are grateful, start a daily practice of gratitude.

Recall the abundant, loving, and pleasant times in your life and be thankful for anything that comes your way, no matter how little. For instance, Emily decides to keep a gratitude notebook, listing three things every day for which she is thankful. She feels happier and more grateful for the moment as she observes a change in perspective while concentrating on the good parts of her life.

Mindfulness-Based Stress Reduction (MBSR): Use mindfulness techniques to develop present-moment awareness and lower stress levels. These techniques include conscious breathing, meditation, and body scan exercises. To promote inner calm and clarity, practice mindfulness by observing thoughts and feelings without being attached in order to promote inner calm and clarity. David, for instance, enrolls in a mindfulness-based stress reduction course where he gains skills for stress management and wellbeing enhancement. He can maintain his composure in the face of adversity because he regularly practices mindfulness, which increases his presence and resilience.

Finding the Crucial Parent and Rebuilding Your Bond

To repent means to acknowledge and change the essential parent within oneself. In this section, we'll examine how to recognize the critical parent voice and replace it with a more compassionate and loving inner voice.

The first stage is to become conscious of the critical inner dialogue that might seem like severe perfectionism, self-criticism, or self-judgment. Observe when the critical voice comes into your mind and how it affects your emotions, ideas, and actions. For example, Sarah recognizes her own voice when she looks in the mirror and hears herself criticizing her appearance. She stops and realizes that this judgment is coming from her critical father and not from herself, rather than accepting it as gospel.

Embracing warped thoughts: Take aim at the skewed viewpoints and assumptions that the critical parent's voice is pushing. Make use of cognitive restructuring strategies to disprove these ideas and substitute more impartial, empathetic beliefs. For instance, Alex questions his critical parents' conviction that he has to do well all the time in order to be deserving of their affection. He disproves this notion by recognizing his intrinsic value, regardless of his accomplishments, and moving toward self-acceptance and self-compassion. Take up self-compassionate hobbies to counter the judgmental voice of your parents. Accept that you are flawed, and that this is a natural part of being human.

When you feel self-conscious or under criticism, give yourself some love and support. Maya often uses self-compassionate responses to her inner critic, such as "I deserve love and acceptance just as I am" and "It's okay to make mistakes; I'm only human." Through self-compassion, she learns how to mend the scars left by her judgmental mother.

Treat your wounded inner child with compassion, since they can face harsh criticism from the critical parent. Calm, soothe, and affirm your inner child to make them feel secure and accepted. For example, John believes that his inner mother is reprimanding him like a little kid. He connects with his inner child in a loving and encouraging way, providing the solace and affirmation he was lacking as a youngster.

Establish boundaries by refusing to participate in the damaging messages sent by the critical parent voice. When the voice of criticism starts to emerge, focus on loving routines and self-compassion. For instance, Emily chooses to put off self-improvement and reflection when she senses that her inner critic is becoming too much. She prioritizes self-care by engaging in fun and soothing activities instead of criticizing herself.

Seek guidance and support from family, close friends, or therapists to gain insight and inspiration on how to modify the important parent-child link. David discusses his issues with self-criticism with his therapist, who assists him in examining the underlying beliefs and attitudes that validate his inner critic.

He learns strategies to cope with the critical parent voice and receives encouragement and support for doing so.

Compassionate Parental Methods and Tools

Developing self-trust is an essential first step in healing and creating a supportive internal environment.

1. Use positive affirmations to boost your self-esteem and believe in your own skills. Say positive affirmations that encourage your strength, value, and perseverance. Give yourself time to assimilate these inspiring ideas. "I believe that I can manage whatever comes my way with grace and resilience" or "I deserve to be loved and accepted exactly as I am" are some statements Sarah can use to start

her day. She keeps repeating these affirmations until her subconscious is filled with them, which increases her confidence and self-assurance.

2. Honoring Oneself—Professionals: Establish and honor your own commitments to show that you are dependable and self-assured. Maintaining these responsibilities—whether they include establishing limits, putting self-care first, or working toward personal objectives—builds your confidence in your capacity to look after yourself. For instance, Alex makes a daily commitment to dedicating time to practices like meditation, physical activity, and creative expression that enhance his well-being. Because he regularly keeps his word, he gains confidence and self-assurance in his ability to prioritize his requests.

3. Reflective Journaling: In a reflective diary, examine and affirm your ideas, emotions, and experiences. Go back to the times in your notebook when you behaved ethically and confidently in yourself. Treat these events as confirmations of your own beliefs. Maya, for instance, records in her notebook the occasions when she followed her gut and made choices that were in line with her general well-being and genuine self. She strengthens her self-assurance by thinking back on these encounters and restating her faith in her own discernment and comprehension.

4. Acquiring mindfulness skills may improve your capacity to interact with inner guidance and intuition. To make decisions that are in line with your beliefs and objectives, you may also

depend on your inner guiding system. Pay attention to the tiny indications that your body and intuition are sending you, and respect these feelings as important sources of information. John, for instance, uses mindfulness meditation as a way to calm his thoughts and strengthen his intuition. He gains confidence in his ability to make choices that are true to himself as he learns to pay attention to the feelings in his body and the guidance from his inner voice.

5. Self-Validation and Compassion: To demonstrate your acceptance and self-trust, engage in self-validation and compassion exercises. Recognize your own ideas, emotions, and experiences with grace and compassion, emphasizing your intrinsic value. For instance, Emily gives herself words of confidence and comfort when she's feeling down by accepting

and validating her feelings without passing judgment. She gains self-assurance and confidence in her emotional fortitude by attesting to her own experiences.

6. Seeking Development and Feedback: Rather than seeing criticism as a negative thing, view it as a chance for personal development. You may use criticism as a driving force for growth and learning if you are confident enough to recognize the difference between helpful and harmful comments. David would ask friends and mentors for their opinions on his creative endeavors because he felt he could assess their comments and apply astute criticism to his work. He feels more respectable and secure in his creative abilities when he accepts criticism as a tool for improvement.

Thinking logically after distortion: a deep path of self-discovery and metamorphosis that promotes inner healing and raises resilience, serenity, and fulfillment.

Start with developing self-acceptance and compassion for yourself. Be kind and sympathetic to yourself, and accept every part of who you are.

Treat yourself with the same empathy you would for a close friend going through a difficult moment. If you're feeling down or self-conscious, try gently telling yourself that "it's okay to feel this way" in order to practice self-compassion. "I am deserving of acceptance and affection, just as I am." Give yourself permission to be empathetic and transparent in order for healing to occur.

Try writing, sketching, or creating art as a way to make a connection with the wounded parts of yourself that may be harboring unresolved grief or trauma from the past. For your inner child to feel secure and welcomed, they want consolation, certainty, and confidence. Close your eyes, for example, and imagine that you are a helpless infant in need of protection and affection.

Talk words of comfort and assurance to this inner kid as you provide it with love and care. The first stages of recovery are acceptance and affirmation, so give yourself permission to mourn whatever hurt and abuse you may have endured.

Letting go of grudges, resentment, and animosity toward oneself and other people is the first step toward healing. Recognize that forgiveness does not imply endorsing misbehavior; rather, it involves letting go of the grief you once gave them. For example, consider old grievances or hurts that caused you great emotional distress.

Realize that by forgiving others, you can end the cycle of suffering and animosity.

Recognize that harboring resentment only makes things worse, and develop the ability to forgive both yourself and other people. Through mindfulness and presence techniques such as breathing exercises, mindful movement, or meditation, you can develop inner calm and clarity while staying anchored in the present moment.

Give yourself permission to live each moment to the fullest with an open mind and curiosity. For instance, schedule some time each day to practice mindful breathing techniques or mindfulness meditation. As you breathe in and out, pay attention to the feelings that firmly ground you in the here and now.

Make the choice to let go of regrets and anxieties about the past in order to concentrate on appreciating how wonderful the present is. With expressive arts therapy, learn how to tap into your subconscious ideas and feelings, examine your moods, and encourage self-expression and creativity. Writing, drawing, or dancing are examples of creative pursuits that may help you express your inner feelings and promote healing. For example, schedule time for writing, sketching, or dancing as creative expression.

Give yourself permission to openly express your feelings using the medium of your choice, without fear of rebuke or condemnation. Have faith in the transformational ability of art to promote self-awareness and healing.

Seek advice, support, and empathy from therapists, family members, or close friends as you embark on your journey of inner recovery. Don't be scared to be upfront and honest about the challenges you are facing, since you are not alone in your journey to recovery. For example, look for a support group or therapist who can help you safely and productively explore your inner experiences.

Tell trusted friends or family about your problems so they can see and hear you in a compassionate and understanding way.

CHAPTER FIVE
BUILDING SELF-HEALING

Acquiring the ability to heal oneself Starting to heal yourself from the inside out is a potent form of self-care and self-discovery that improves people's emotional equilibrium, serenity, and sense of fulfillment. In this section, we'll cover a variety of techniques and approaches that support internal healing and enhance self-relationships.

Thankfulness and self-acceptance

To develop self-acceptance and self-compassion, start by accepting and appreciating who you are. Recognize that you deserve love and compassion in spite of your previous transgressions and flaws. When confronted with tough emotions or situations, you might tell yourself things like, "I am doing the best I can right now" or "It's okay to

struggle; I am worthy of love and acceptance."
Treat yourself with the same compassion that you
would show to a dear friend in distress.

Healing of the Inner Child

Analyze your inner child's hurtful places through
writing, reflection, or visualization activities.
Being present for the younger versions of yourself
who may still be carrying unresolved trauma or
suffering, and offering support and affirmation can
help. For example, close your eyes and picture
yourself as a defenseless little kid in need of care
and protection. Gently and compassionately
address any sadness or anguish you have while
keeping this picture in your mind's eye. Comfort
and uplift your inner child with words of support
to help them feel secure and welcomed.

Letting go and forgiving

Develop the capacity to let go of grudges, anger, and bitterness toward both other people and oneself. Recognise that letting go of the past and forgiving yourself is a gift you give yourself. Consider, for example, any old grudges or resentments that are causing you a lot of emotional anguish. Not only do you acknowledge the hurt they have caused you, but also the liberation you will have when you forgive them. Since forgiveness is a potent tool for self-compassion and healing, extend it to both yourself and other people.

Being present and mindful

Cultivating presence and mindfulness may be achieved by breathing exercises, meditation, or conscious awareness. It's critical to stay in the now and give oneself permission to live life to the fullest, most fascinating, and most genuine of possibilities. Set aside a certain period of time each day to practice mindfulness techniques like mindful breathing or meditation. With every breath in and breath out, pay attention to the sensations of your breath, as they help you return to the present moment. Let go of regrets for the past and worries for the future in order to fully experience the richness of the present.

Expression of the Arts and Self-Discovery

Through creative expression, one might develop self-awareness through dance, music, or literature. Give yourself permission to access your inner creative and intuitive abilities as you use art as a tool for healing and self-transformation. For example: Schedule some time each week to work on a creative project that makes you happy, such as writing, drawing, dancing, or playing music. Put your faith in the wisdom and insight that come from artistic investigation, and use the medium of your choice to communicate your ideas.

Seeking support and connection

Seek out therapists, family members, or trustworthy friends who can provide support, understanding, and direction throughout your recovery process. Recognize that you are not alone in your quest for inner healing, and don't be embarrassed to talk about your shortcomings. Consider, for example, going to therapy or joining a support group as a safe space to share your inner experiences. When you tell the people who matter most to your well-being about your struggles and successes, you will get encouragement and affirmation from them.

Searching for your inner love nest

Taking care of your love nest inside Establishing an atmosphere of kindness and compassion inside yourself is the first step toward developing emotional wellbeing and self-compassion. This section will cover several techniques and approaches to help us create a secure, warm, and inviting interior.

Develop self-compassion

To begin with, treat yourself with kindness, empathy, and encouragement while you're going through challenging times or unpleasant situations. Treat yourself with the same decency and attention that you would a close friend or relative. When you're having a hard time or feeling depressed, sayings like "It's okay to struggle; I am here for myself" or "May I be gentle with myself in this moment of difficulty" might help cheer you up. Recognize your worth and accept your flaws in a kind and perceptive manner.

Secondly, provide a safe area for yourself where you may communicate your ideas, emotions, and desires without worrying about criticism or reprisals. Permit yourself to be genuine and truthful with yourself. Be kind to your inner self. Set aside some time each day, for example, to write in your journal or to reflect on your feelings and ideas. Give yourself a space free from judgment so that you may compassionately and curiously explore your inner terrain, knowing that every aspect of you is respected and appreciated. Taking care of your body, mind, and soul via self-care routines is essential to developing a whole, healthy sense of who you are. You may respect your need for rest and renewal by doing things that make you happy, satisfied, and relaxed. Set aside some time each day for pursuits like yoga, reading, listening to music, or taking a stroll outdoors that will boost your energy and mood. To keep your inner sanctuary intact, you need to take care of yourself. Pay attention to what your body needs, and treat it with the respect it deserves.

Take on an attitude of appreciation and thankfulness. Develop an attitude of appreciation and thankfulness for all the benefits and prosperity in your life. This will bring you inner contentment and fulfillment. Embrace each moment with wonder and appreciation, focusing on the kindness and beauty all around you. For instance, set aside some time every day to think about the things you have to be thankful for, including the simple things in life, the feel of the sun on your skin, or the laughter of loved ones. Developing an attitude of gratitude may make you feel better and more content. Realize how fortunate you are. Be clear and forceful about your boundaries in your interactions with others while respecting your needs, values, and limitations. Maintain an atmosphere of positivity and inspiration around you to prevent negativity and toxicity from entering your inner refuge. Prioritizing your needs and objectives may be practiced, for example, by saying no to obligations and pursuits that sap your energy or jeopardize your well-being. As you identify as a kind but strong defender of yourself, setting boundaries is a sign of self-care and self-respect.

In the event that you are embarking on a path of self-exploration and recovery, seek the guidance, comprehension, and validation of therapists, family members, or trustworthy friends. Since you are not alone in your search for inner peace and satisfaction, you may feel comfortable discussing your challenges as well as your victories. Consider attending counseling sessions or joining a support group to make connections with others who have gone through similar struggles and experiences. Allow the people who really care about your well-being to encourage and validate you when you divulge specifics of your inner journey.

CONCLUSION

To begin the journey of inner healing and building a loving inner home requires courage and change. Throughout our research, we have looked at a variety of methods and strategies meant to support emotional health, self-compassion, and inner calm.

By engaging in self-compassion practices, we may learn to embrace and understand who we are, as well as our inherent worth and value. By allowing us to embrace our thoughts, feelings, and goals without judgment or criticism, creating a safe space for self-expression encourages openness and genuineness.

We can take care of our body, mind, and soul when we are aware of our well-being. Additionally, it supports the development of appreciation and thankfulness, which widens our hearts to the abundance and beauty that surround us.

Setting healthy boundaries gives us the ability to protect our inner sanctuary from negativity and toxicity, which gives us a sense of self-worth and empowerment. Asking trustworthy friends, family members, or therapists for support and guidance also provides us with empathy, validation, and guidance on our journey to healing and self-discovery.

May we never lose sight of the fact that, as we recognize our loving inner home, healing is a lifelong process of growth, self-discovery, and transformation. With each stride we take toward inner serenity and completion, may we uncover more fortitude, empathy, and integrity inside ourselves, creating a sanctuary where we feel incredibly loved, valued, and at home.

A REVISION OF "THE LOVING PARENT GUIDEBOOK" WAS REQUESTED

Would you please, reader? Hopefully, you're doing well as I write this. By name, I'm Joyful Bofest, and I wrote ***"The Loving Parent Guidebook."*** I would be grateful if you would consider sharing your thoughts and observations. I'm contacting you in order to request a book review.

"The Loving Parent Guidebook" focuses on the intricate interactions between emotionally immature parents and adult children and offers helpful advice on overcoming aloof, rejecting, or self-absorbed parental relationships. With the use of personal tales, psychological understandings, and therapeutic techniques, the book provides readers with a roadmap for reparenting and establishing deep connections with both themselves and other people.

Some of the main ideas covered in the book are as follows: The influence of emotionally immature parents on the lives of their adult offspring is examined in the book Discovering Your Inner Teenage.

We may get a better understanding of emotional immaturity by examining the characteristics and consequences of emotional immaturity in caregivers.

Encouraging Inner Healing: Offering techniques and approaches to promote mental health and self-acceptance.

Establishing trust involves providing techniques and materials to enhance self-confidence and self-belief.

Creating a Safe and Comforting Inner Environment:

Examining Techniques for Establishing a Safe and Comforting Inner Environment. Your knowledge and viewpoint, in my opinion, would significantly enhance the conversation on this crucial subject. With your review, prospective readers can assess the book's worth and consider how it relates to their own experiences.

If you would like to review "The Loving Parent

Guidebook," I will provide you with a copy at no extra cost in the format of your choice. Tell me the postal address or email address you would like sent, please.

I appreciate your consideration of my plea. I value your attention and time, and I'm excited to speak with you.

Sincerely,